"I read the poems and found all of them good. Every poem has an emotional reality. This is rarely found in modern poetry which is only cerebral."

Prof. M. Krishnan Nair
(Literary critic and orator)

MIRACLE MIX

A REPOSITORY OF POEMS

MIRACLE MIX

A REPOSITORY OF POEMS

N M K

ZORBA BOOKS

Published in India by Zorba Books, 2016

Website: www.zorbabooks.com
Email: info@zorbabooks.com

ISBN Print Book - 978-93-85020-82-7
ISBN eBook – 978-93-85020-83-4

Zorba Books Pvt. Ltd.(opc)
Gurgaon, INDIA

DEDICATED
To
the Holy Trinity
And
Ginu, Josh, Yash
and
my parents

ACKNOWLEDGEMENTS

To the late professor M. Krishnan Nair who sieved through many of my poems and encouraged me to continue writing poetry.

To those who prayed for my success.

To all my teachers.

To Zulfi, Arathy and all my friends who made me believe that I am a poet.

PREFACE

I believe that these poems were gifted to me over the years by the word which came from the mouth of the creator.

William Wordsworth said, "*Poetry is the spontaneous overflow of powerful feelings : it takes its origin from emotions recollected in tranquility.*" For me, poems are expressions of reminiscences and schemes of life, a world we once were in and a world where we wish to be.

It is the poetic gust which lends shape to imagination and helps in weaving words to convey plain emotions that we go through every day. I feel blessed that this gust impregnated me with poetic diction.

- NMK

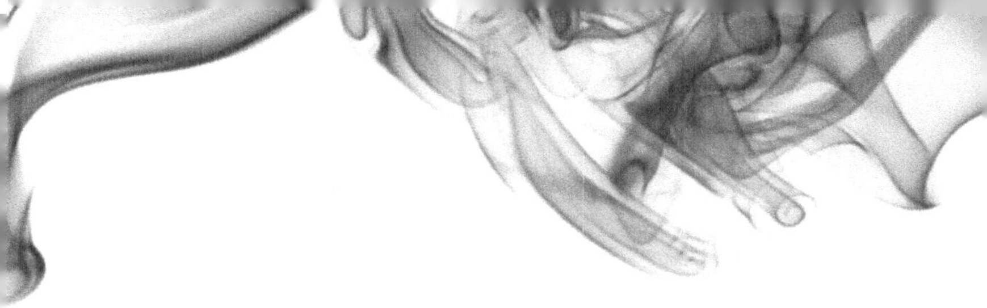

Content

HUMOUR

NARRATIVES

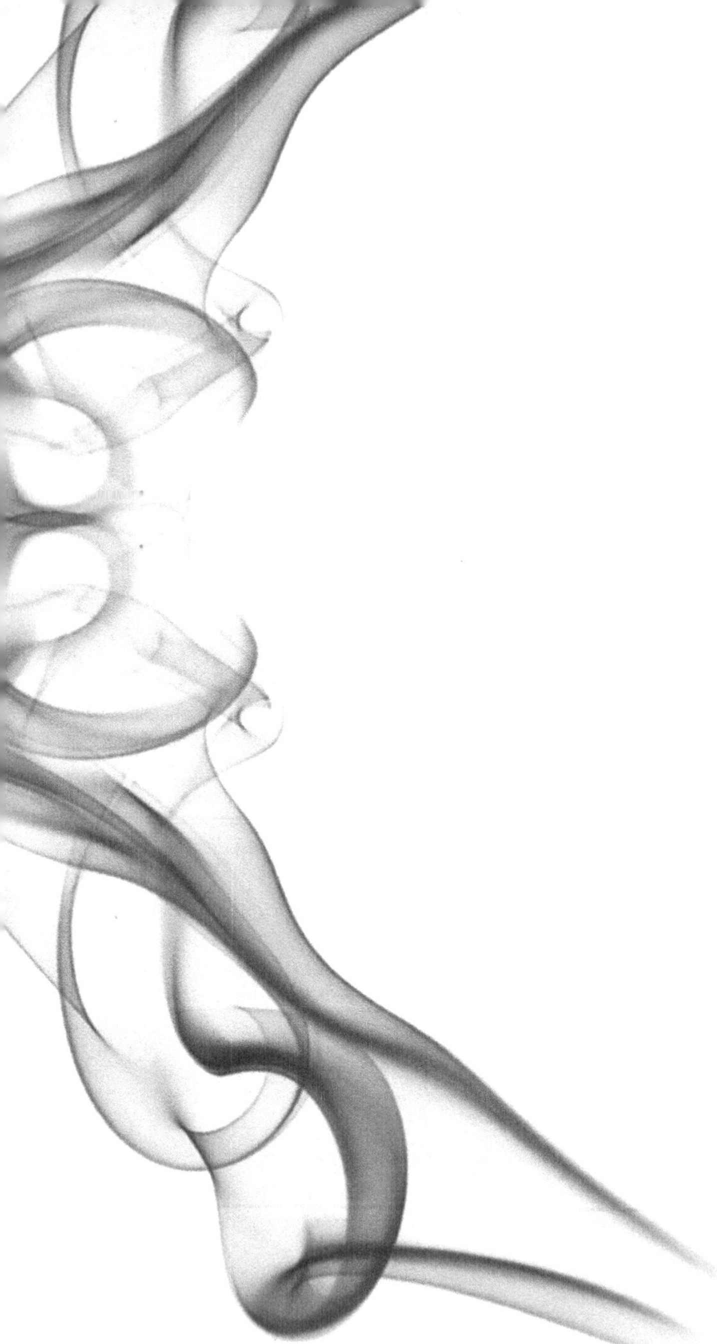

TOURING
CLOUDS

Wonder where the white ships go
Sailing calmly on the deep blue sky.
Are they in quest of something
Or on a tour of our earth?

Moving over the hamlets and fields,
Form they a shield for the layman below.
Move they in ranks, as the kite
Flying beside, peep into the vessel.

As they journey, they draw maps
And images of well- known characters.
With the evening sky as back-drop
Conjure they magic to savour.

The sails are brought down
As the wind retires from its work.
The anchor is dropped on the mountain,
And the clouds form a majestic crown.

Enchanting it must be to witness
The green earth as a bird's view.
Permission I seek to step aboard,
Wonder who steereth thee, cumulus.

THE FISHERMAN AND THE SEA

Why thou rage, my sea?
Weren't you calm all day?
Is thine anger with me?
Have I displeased you, say?

You're no longer at peace
And thy replica above darkens.
Feared tempest gathers to tease,
My vessel suffers all that happens.

You toss up my little boat,
Her planks no longer hold.
You gave what I sought,
My thatch, now allow me to behold.

Fear thou not, humble voyager,
Not that I misinterpreted you.
Thrilled was I, pardon the err,
But I do have on you my view

Excited was I as sky shadowed
'Cause clouds are ready to rain.
Tidings and news of heaven are awaited
And the droplets bring it fain.

Go thy way now, fisherman,
I give you my assuring vow.
My regards take to thine woman,
And for thee to pass, I bow.

HER PRETTY LITTLE FROCK

Stark naked stood she,
The little cherry tree,
Her pretty little frock stolen.
Autumn has robbed her apparel
Once gifted by the spring,
Later embroidered by summer.

Jade green was her embellished frock
With a brown lining at hem.
Deep red hearts adorned it
With some beautiful flowers sprinkled.
Alluring it was in design
And ravishing when in motion.

Lo! Here she stands embarrassed
By the atrocity of autumn.
Tease her not, ogle her never.
Winter has promised her a coat
One white unblemished spread
Till spring arrives with a new.

THE MOON

I will be there to appreciate, when
The moon luminates the earth
And stars illuminate the sky,
Besides the watery ribbon
To witness the above man's
Narcissism, and old dish he is.

Maybe he's deciphering the secret,
For a strange beauty he has.
Maybe worrying over, for
Hath he no human features.
Or could be tidying the face,
Before resuming his journey.

A plaintive solo draws near,
It's the boatman, home bound.
Stop, ferryman! For the ripples
From your floater disturbs.
Allow him alone, the old man,
Let him ponder or powder.

TO A BUTTERFLY

Colourful of all the creatures
And delicate of them all,
From where thou got these colours?
Hast thou bought them from
The bearded old artist?

From the ugliest, thou made
Thyself the most sought of all.
From where thou got these colours?
Hast thou borrowed them from
The cheerful arched rainbow?

Like a queen thou roam
Sprinkling happiness all around.
From where thou got these colours?
Hast thou got it while gathering
The nectar from the blooming flowers?

Winged creature of hues
Sweetest of all coalescence,
From where thou got these colours?
Reveal thy secret and allow me
Add some colour to this grey life.

COWS

They were a haughty pair of cows,
Munching beside the yellow cowslips,
Incising the creeper's red cowberry,
Rifting the long pods of cowpea
But leaving alone the umber of cowbane
Deemed to be scarier than cowpox.

Then came a locomotive armouring a cowcatcher,
Rumbling, clamouring, hooting, it cowed.
They, who were grazing, cowered,
Hither and thither ran like cowards
Ringing on their necks the cowbells.
Behind them scrambled the cowherd
His tuft of oily hair cowlicked,
Treading on the fresh green cow dung
Leaping over the hedge of cow parsley
Brandishing all the way his cow whip.

THE QUARRY

A little way is quarry
Where men toil, nought worry
From dawn till dusk,
For it's their task.

By the hill so gawky
Is a pool full, much murky.
'It was a ditch,' they say
'Till rains filled it last May.'

In it swim little fish
Seldom used as a dish.
No one knows how they got there,
Indeed it's something queer.

For herons, it's their haunt
And crows loiter around.
Tired men refresh in it,
Stray dogs jump and hit.

Often a cry can be heard,
One that warns all the crowd.
Then there will be a scurry
As everyone for shelter hurry.

No men are seen around
Nor crows that are abound
Herons are quick to flee,
Dogs scamper with a plea.

Anxious moments pass very slow,
As everyone awaits the blow.
Soon the dynamite will burst
Rocks, splinters fly past.

When all is at peace
Workmen go back to their piece
And the rest for their loll
Till heard is another yell.

THE NOON WIND

Wait for me, chirping birds,
Soon I will return to hear you,
For I got an errand.
The yeoman yonder the hill
Hath a big yoke to work.
Waits he for his beloved,
For she bringeth his refreshment
To him I should herald,
The glad time of rest.

Let compassion overcometh duty.
So allow me time, feathers,
Before he resumeth the plough,
To embrace him a little,
And cool his poor soul.
Then cometh I to hear music,
Which soothes my inner core.
Till then await on this bough,
Thou blissful hearts.

THE CRY OF MOTHER EARTH

They are my offspring,
Everything under my glare.
Made I man among them,
Superior, far above others.
Regretting I am now, this 'cause

Everything he asked, I gave.
Arrogant is this son,
Own affairs does not he mind,
Troubling my egoless children
And making them extinct.

I've warned and coaxed.
My children's houses, tramples he,
And makes his own palaces.
Spewing poison onto my face,
He poisons his own food.

His wastes of destruction pollute,
Making his own offspring retard.
The lilies of the valley cry,
Pointing to the dried dead stumps
And place where life once flowed.

I've lived happily this far
And now have wishes no more,
Time is ripe to open my volcanoes,
But yet wait, if he shall return,
That prodigal son of mine.

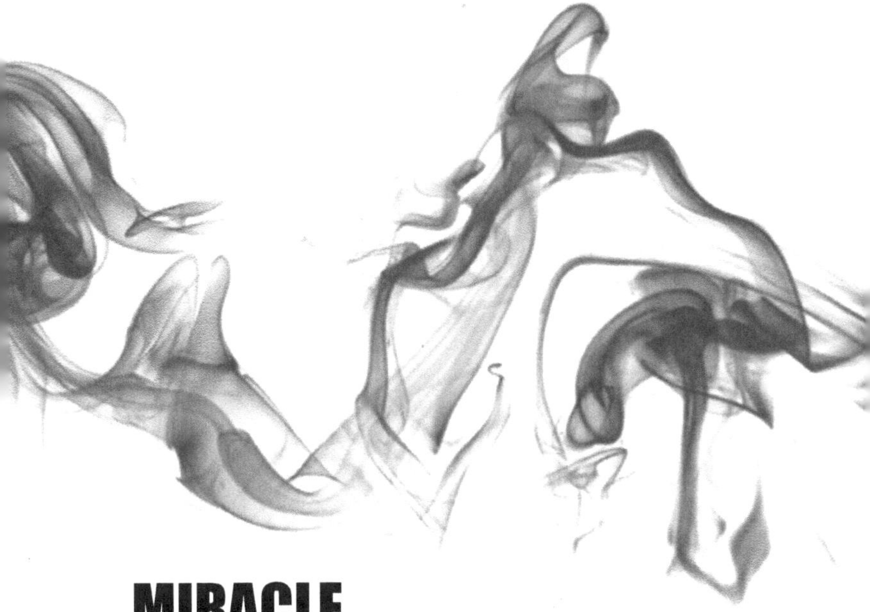

MIRACLE MIX

My knowledge grew thus.
My teacher pointing to the east said,
"That's where the sun starts his work."
And turning to the west continued,
"That's where it goes to rest."
Then pointing to the north, she said,
"That's where the mountains are,"
And turning towards the south continued,
"That's where the seas are."
Then holding my hand, she said,
"Below there is gravity
Keeping you firmly on earth
And above is the Almighty,
To care for you on the way."

THE GREAT HUMANS

Great are we, humans,
For we conquered the summits high
And reached the poles distant,
To know the distance precise.
Oh! How wonderful we are.

Great are we, humans,
For we measured the ocean fathomless
And dug into earth's core
To know what treasure there lies.
Oh! How curious we are.

Great are we, humans,
For we traversed the forests dark
And treaded the worlds distant,
To widen our knowledge.
Oh! How brave we are.

Great are we, miserable humans,
For we learned the things strangest
And discovered the unknown,
Yet are foolish not to understand
A poor needy soul beside.

THOUGHTS OF A SUICIDER

How should it be?
One self-inflicted bite of the reptile,
Just like done by the Egyptian princess!
But then isn't it paining?
And all my life has pained enough.

How should it be?
A self-concocted poison of exotic herbs,
Just like done by the great Greek philosopher!
But then isn't it bitter?
And all my life was bitter enough.

How should it be?
A self-imposed pierce with a dagger,
Just like done by the cornered proud warriors!
But then isn't it bloody?
And all my life has bled enough.

How should it be?
A self-lightened fire burning red,
Just like done by Rajput widows!
But then isn't it charring?
And all my life has charred enough.

How should it be?
A self-tied knot embracing the neck,
Just like done by the inseparable lovers!
But then isn't it choking?
And all my life has choked enough.

How should it be?
A self-posed question with no answer,
Just like done by own grey life!
But then isn't life to be led?
And all my life has been misled.

How should it be, I know
A self-found answer to the question,
Just like done by a brave honourable loser!
To start again afresh,
With bright smile, like of a newborn.

THE SEEKER

To know what is this world
That encompasses his fold,
A hermit in quest of heights
Journeyed to view the world below.
He walked on to be fulfilled.

Touring he saw a flagpole
On which fluttered the pride.
Climbed on it, hermit, to view below
And saw the multitude striding.
He climbed down fulfilled.

Treading along into a grove
He chose the tallest of trees.
Climbed on it, hermit, to view below
And saw the greenery spread out.
He climbed down fulfilled.

Journeying he reached a minaret
Weathering centuries of last ten.
Climbed on it, hermit, to view below
And saw the architectural glory around.
He climbed down fulfilled.

Moving on took him to the shore
Where the helpful lighthouse towered.
Climbed on it, hermit, to view below
And saw the deep blue sea stretch.
He climbed down fulfilled.

Thinking this was the world
Encompassing him and the fold
He turned to his ashram
To sprinkle on his disciples
The wisdom of the world.

Then an enormous mountain
Barred the path of the seeker.
Climbed on it, hermit, to view below
And saw nothingness, haze all around.
He climbed down perplexed.

Walking on, he laughed abruptly
For his journey was worth.
Ran on now, hermit, to share the truth
For he had been enlightened.
This whole world is maya.

PREY

Never did the fly know,
The little volant insect,
Of the warty toad
Waiting patiently for him.

And never did the toad know,
The round cold amphibian,
Of the slithering snake
Moving calmly up to him

And never did the snake know,
The long tattooed reptile,
Of the eyeing eagle
Swooping gently up to him.

And never did the eagle know,
The large spanning avian,
Of the predator man
Aiming silently at him.

And never, never did the man know,
The always wise mammal,
Of the treacherous fellow man
Drawing quietly his dagger behind.

GROWING UP

In my childhood –

Five mangoes for five rupees,
To the market my mother sent me
And I bought for her as she said.

In my teens -
Five mangoes for five rupees,
To the market my mother sent me.
I bought her three and said,
'Oh! How the prices are spiralling.'

Later in life -
Five mangoes for five rupees
To the market my mother sent me.
I returned her ten ripe
Along with the five rupees.

-This must be growing up-

(The price of mangoes is supposed to be
constant throughout the period)

THE TENTH GAZE

Men have gazes to dwell upon.
Upward gaze to God when in need
And downwards in fear,
Laterally they gaze enviously
And medially to frown.

In the upward medial angle
They gaze to think,
To upward lateral angle in dream.
In the downward medial angle
They gaze to regret,
To downward lateral angle in sorrow.

Into oblivion they look straight
And no gaze in anger, he is blind.
Together nine gazes have many
But the tenth, only few.

It's the in-gaze,
Gaze which gets reflected
So deep in mind
To beam forth out
As fore – gaze; wisdom.

REVOLUTION

(Let air reverberate with speech,
Let blood ripple till it spills over)

Revolutions are
to happen
For leaders to be born.
Powers are bestowed on,
to serve,
But will be misused,
Some even to dictate.

Thus a criminal is born
To corrupt the
entire system,
A society lot has
dreamed,
For which many
strained.
So commoners
will gather,
A gatherer with hope amid,
For revolutions are
to happen.

THE PERPLEXING NAME

Boon companion of man,
Enchanting but pestering,
Loquacious yet serene,
Constructed from a rib
Of a man slumbering.
How should we spell
Your perplexing name?

Woo – man?
Wooing the way through,
The easiest of paths,
For you mastered the art
Oh! Woo, Woo, Woo – man,
Is this how you spell?

Vow – man?
Vows are a compulsion
To satisfy your inner being
And you nag for it.
How! Vow, Vow, Vow – man,
Is this how you spell?

Wow – man?
Wow is the exclamation
When attired to charm
You so wish to hear.
Ho! Wow, Wow, Wow – man,
Is this how you spell?

Woe – man?
Woe is the companion
Cast beside you
And tears a resort.
Ho! Woe, Woe, Woe – man,
Is this how you spell?

Boon companion of man
Enchanting but pestering,
Loquacious yet serene,
Loving and devoted,
Constructed from a rib
Of a man slumbering.
It's a name you have
And a logic for it
Can turn heady a logician.

RELUCTANT DEATHS

And the female was born
And the midwife frustrated.
And she wrung the tender neck
And a reluctant death ensued.
Death of morality.

And the female grew
And the heinous winked.
And she lay there plundered
And a reluctant death ensued.
Death of humanity.

And the female became a bride
And the bridegroom was in greed.
And she was charred forever
And a reluctant death ensued.
Death of mentality.

And the female in wedlock
And her spouse on pyre.
And she sat on it doomed
And a reluctant death ensued.
Death of spirituality.

And the female when fatigued
And the knell echoed,
And she greeted it gleaming
And a willing death ensued.
Death of flesh.

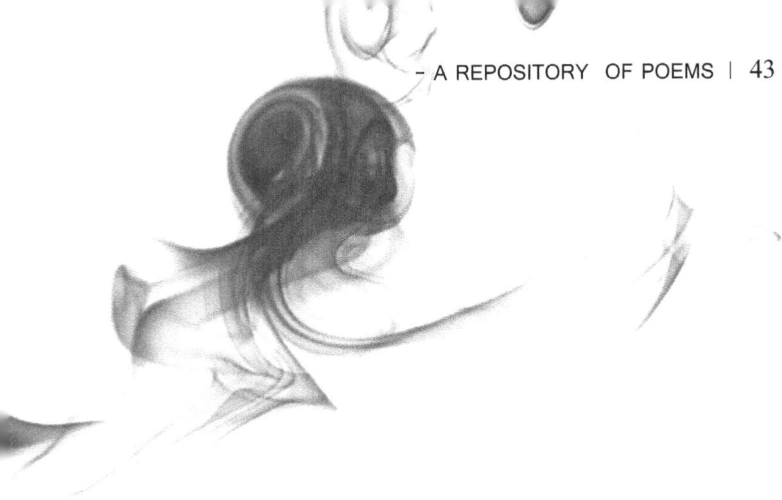

FEATHERS

Wish I were a kite,
To spy the below earth
From that dizzying height
While holding little children's breath
As I glide on the winds.

Wish I were a nightingale,
To sing aloud in the woods
From an old trunk, without fail,
While beholding the nature's moods
As I mesmerise the simple spirits.

Wish I were a swan,
To swim beside the lotus,
From a bud to an older one
While commenting on irregular banks
As I paddle lightly along the flow.

Wish I were a peacock,
To bring out those thousand eyes
From that tail, a colourful frock
While fluttering, inviting envies
As I dance to the rhythm of rain.

Wish I were an albatross,
To wander out to the farthest island
Away from these frenzied crowds
While feeling the powerful trade wind
As I sweep gently over the sea.

Wish I were a phoenix,
To speed myself into a fire
From this stagnant life, a vex,
While the flames form a pyre
As I rush in, to be born again.

LIFE

Squatting under
golden sun,
Letting brine
kiss my feet,
Let I,
my mind along the horizon,
To know what's life.

My mind roams over,
By finding the fathomless
sea drift
With its scaly hungry creatures,
Eightieth and score on left.
On the other side exhaling fire,
Dragon and serpents
in darkness leapt.

Careful,
cautions my mind,
Awfully thin this rim is.
One stray step,
you end,
On which side,
never matters.

THE SINNER

Why thou drizzle?
Oh! Goddess of rain.
Come down hard
On this weakling,
To purge my sins,
And to cleanse.

Regretting my actions
I await thee,
Baring my chest.
Pour thine relish
To relieve me.
Hold thyself not.

Drained of life
Now I stand
Under clouds heavy,
To wet my tongue
And to renew life,
For I'm a sinner.

WOMAN

Strange art thou.......woman,

Strangeness.......thy beauty.

Strangely.......thou behave

Stranger.........am I to thine world.

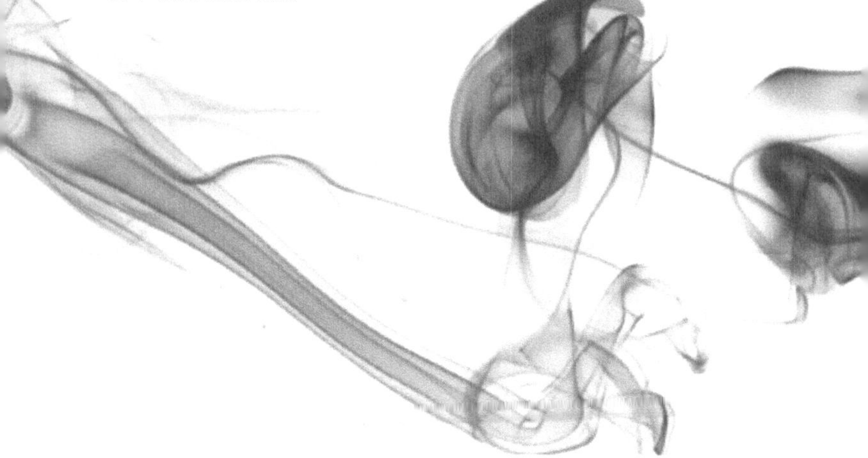

HANDFUL OF THORNS

To wrench the blooming roses,
To wander around a mysterious cactus,
To irk a porcupine so precarious,
All ends in a handful of thorns.

The one who adorns a throne,
The peasant who fumingly drones,
The mortals who are death prone,
All complain of handful of thorns.

For the saviour prince, crown full of thorns,
For the banished prince, bed full of thorns,
For the renounced prince, feet full of thorns,
And listen we commoners,
least is this handful of thorns.

BARRENNESS

In a barrenly dry month of the year,
In a land romanced by barrenness,
Is a barren woman of dark hue
Tying her barren cow of darker tint
To a barren tree so fragile
On which was a barren nest
Occasioned by a barren quail
Flying below the barren clouds
Which roamed under the barren sky
Which enveloped this so barren land
Where a curse called barrenness roamed
Much to the woe of the woman,
A barren woman of dark hue
Tying her barren cow of darker tint
To a barren tree so fragile
On which was a barren nest
Occasioned ....

RED

She stood beside
An yellow lamp lit ,
He walked over
With green eyes lit.
Besides were tenements
Lights of white sparsely lit.
Up above were celestials,
All of them silvern lit.
Everything takes place
In a place condemned red-lit.

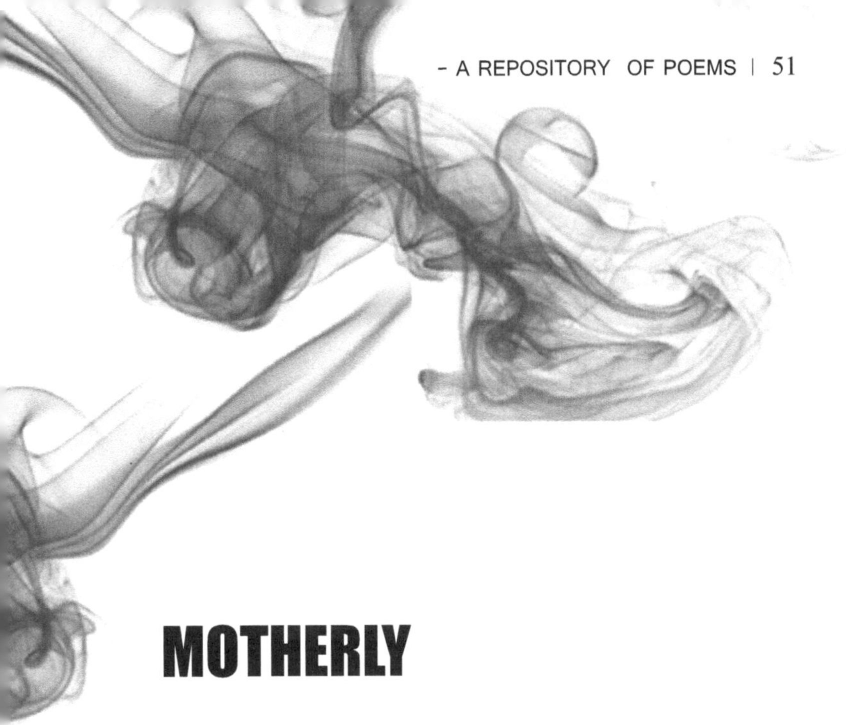

MOTHERLY

Nothing ever mattered to her.
The enormous sound of the mail
As it rushed right behind her,
Neither the mooing of the cow
Nor did she listen to bickerings
Of the slothful neighbours
And she didn't hear the thunder
Heralding a grand shower.
Nothing drew her attention. Why?
Ha, ha, ha
She was deaf.
But then she ran,
Off like an uneasy doe
Into the thatched hut
Hearing her child wail.
B ... bu.... but wasn't she deaf!?

CUR

Be thou a cur,
Pronounced, all in all.
So littered was I,
Under the bad omen,
To loiter and loll.
Man's pride should I be,
But turned his foe,
'Cause, I was omitted
In a shady lane,

Battling sores of soul
And flesh I grew
Amongst other lorns
To a complete loon.
A morsel, I await,
But pelts he stones,
When blessed of our kind
Feast from the very palm,
And my eyes flood when
The fortunate of us
Blend with the youth

Bruised I many
To avenge my birth
Then came the penal
Of highest order.
Fled I to corners
To drag my story.
But now bruises of life
Have destroyed my will.
Sorrowfully now I peep
Into the embellished world,
As it walks past me.
Only if I had a boon,
To spare a little love,
To this cur by the mighty.

BYGONE DAYS

Gone are the days, friend,
When we played in the puddle
And built houses of mud
To play parents and neighbours,
Only to get scabies.

Gone are the days, friend,
When we swam the river
And we attacked the house of crabs
With nothing, but with bare hands,
Only to get the bites.

Gone are the days, friend,
When we climbed the neighbour's trees
And fled with their dog on our heels
Without caring about the fences,
Only to get the bruises.

Gone are the days, friend,
When we dressed ourselves
And sat behind the maidens
To pull on their plaited hair,
Only to hear the unexpected.

Gone are the days, friend,
When we fought with each other
And tore our dresses
Without knowing the real cause,
Only to get the canings.

Gone are the days, friend,
When life was pleasant
And happiness overflowed the brim
Without knowing the burdens of life,
Only to face it later.

DOWN THE RIVER

I've caught the vessel for the hundredth time,
Signaling with a hoot its moment prime
When the young sun warmly smile,
It's eagerness to drift down the mile
Of the old curvaceous green river

I've seen for the hundredth time,
The white crane with its young mime
Staring into the sparkling water
And an occasional elephant, splatter
As a naughty, little child.

I've witnessed for the hundredth time
Priests in water chant a rhyme,
To come out healthier in deeds
While far down a black man chides
His ever stubborn buffalo to turn around.

I've tried for the hundredth time,
To lift out a flower which is fine
Accompanying the mortal remains with woes
As the river vibrates with echoes
Of the stout dhobi's beatings.

I've watched for the hundredth time,
Ladies splashing with gossips in no aim,
Even forgetting the household chore,
Besides an old stooping grey beggar
Slurping to quench his wishes.

I've journeyed the hundredth time
Along this way, always the same,
With its same old pattern.
But to me it's a new yarn
Just like the new face of the old sun.

ALWAYS

To smell the flower
In all its splendour,
And to feel the warmth of love
By filling in me its odour.
Is always my love.

To caress the breeze
With a gentle kiss,
And to know its ease
As it brushes me with a hiss,
Is always my love.

To touch the brook
Running over the pebbles,
And to hear the frog's croak
With the bursting of bubbles,
Is always my love.

To lie on the pastures
As the cattle grazes on,
And to admire its gestures
Under the evening sun,
Is always my love.

To admire the world
In all its beauty,
And to be enough bold
To fulfil my duty,
Is always my love.

IN MY GRANDMA'S BACKYARD

In my Grandma's backyard
Quite near the boundary hedge
Stood a huge tamarind
A resort to many kinds.

On the branch that leaned
Beyond the hedge, dwelled
The melodious quails, inciting
Envy in the crows so hoarse
That bickerings were often
Over a seeming boundary
Attributed to a hedge so low.

Over the crooked branch
That had the greenest leaves
Dashed the naughty squirrels
Dropping the seeds from the pods
On the saint of snakes,
A lousy rat snake, lodging
In the field mice's hole.

On the fat big trunk
At a height so dizzying
Worked the busy woodpecker
Making rooms for settlers new.

At noon came the heron to chat
After a long standstill in the pool
With a fish in its beak to share.

In a hole somewhere
On this huge spreading tree
Lived a demon from myths
To frighten the neighbours' brats.
And on nights of a moon full
Those bats are seen hovering
To rouse one's fear of spirits.

On a dried old twig
Yet strong not to fall
Sat the old owl sleeping
After a keen watch of night
Whom none dared disturb.
Not the quails nor the squirrels.
Not the pecker nor the demon.

This huge tamarind, a resort,
Is no more now, only remains its stump.
For when my Grandma passed
The tree was felled
To char her remains,
Leaving many homeless
And the world shadeless.

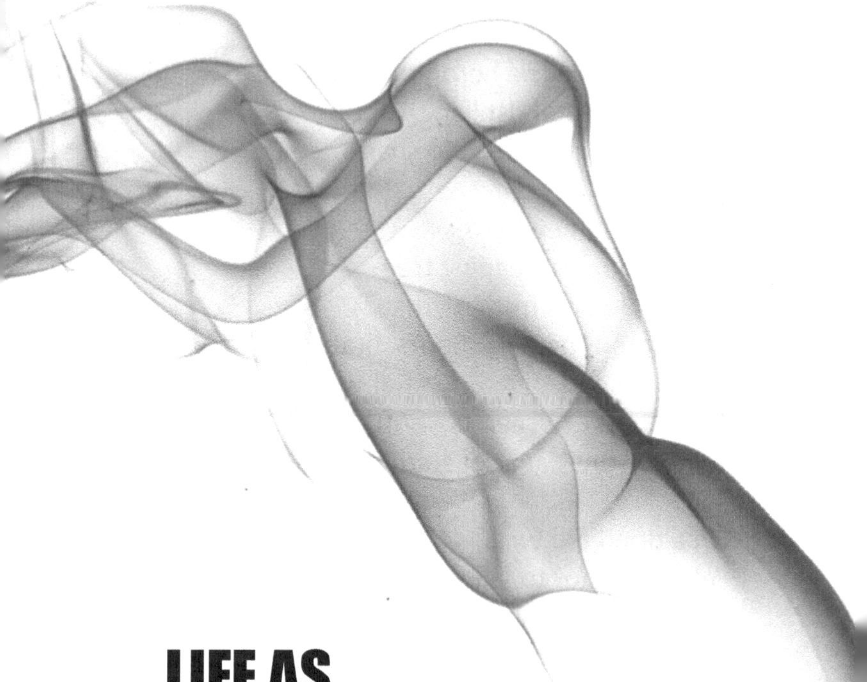

LIFE AS A CLOCK

A big clock is this world
And mere minutes are we,
Living perhaps to sixty
Which tick in a haste.
When the big hand of Almighty
Graces past, one perishes.
Some cherished as some moments are
While others forgotten forever.
Thus when His hand and mind
Finish that big circle,
A generation comes to an end
And his work turns to another.

HISTORY ON A PEDESTAL

History, such an adamant lady,
Coaxes, reprimands her husband Future,
To create stories for her
That she etches on her as her story.

And so happens incidents or accidents,
Murder and birth, freedom yet slavery,
War per treaty, invention plus discoveries
Which she preserves as her story.

Damn beautiful she is amongst the stories,
Attuned to glory as an ancient mother.
Folks flock to her for enrichment,
She whispers what no medium or sorcerer can.

Realise that what she has recorded
Is his creativity, his story and not hers.
Aptly she named herself History,
And we bemused to see her on a pedestal.

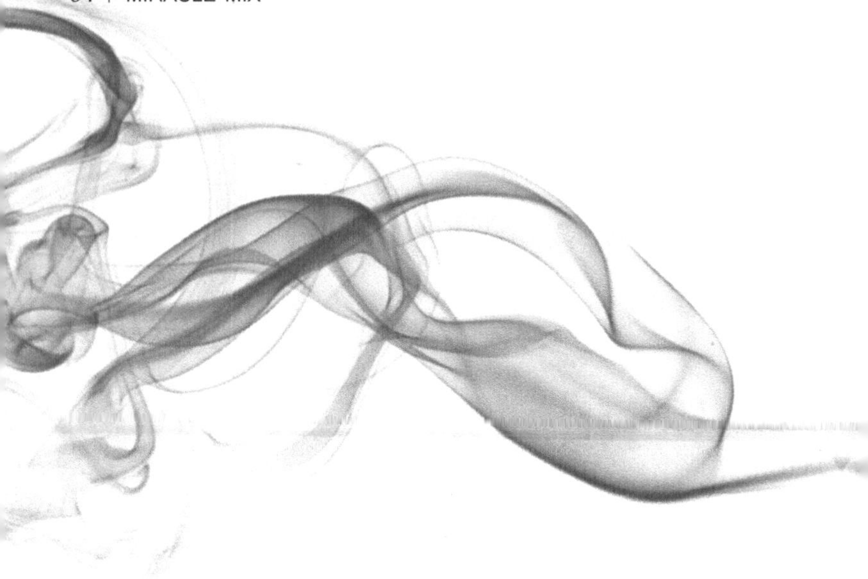

GENESIS

Before man the papers did fly
And before them his mind.
Before his mind the birds flew
And before them the leaves.
Before the leaves the clouds flew
And before them the wind.
Before the wind the time flew
And before it the Holy Spirit,
Over the face of desolate waters
To conjure things desired
For an exquisite world,
A dream of His
Which did fly first,
Cause of us and the entirety.

OLD LITTLE LOST DREAM

On a noble night, stately entirety,
Standing alone, counting stars,
I saw an old slender yellow man
His golden hair plaited
His silver beard knotted,
Rowing the crescent white moon
Through the deep blue sky.
His glittering net he cast
And all the clouds were caught,
But he let them go one by one.
His glittering net he hurled once more
And all the stars were trapped,
But he let them go one by one.
His glittering net he tossed out again
And all the comets were prisoned,
But he let them go one by one.

Surprised by this action so strange
I cried out to the sky,
"Who are you, Yellow old man?
What is it you seek?"
Down came a resounding voice,
"I am a dreamer dreaming,
Dreaming for an old little lost dream."
Mystified, I blinked at his answer
As the old slender yellow man
His golden hair plaited,
His silver beard knotted,
Rowing the crescent white moon
Through the deep blue sky
Called out for his old little lost dream
As he moved along pitching his net.

STARRY LOVE

Why thou wink at me
Night after night,
Stars of heavenly meadows,
Thou daughters of old moon,
Are thou in love with me?

Your gleaming look I adore
Following me to the nooks
And your care for me
Makes me feel wanted.
When thou light the heavens
By night, remember,
You lighten my life too.
Little jewels that adorn
The dark robe, carry me away,
If you love me so,
To your pastures
To sparkle among you.

Fairy creatures, be careful
Let thine mother not know
About our affection.
But she already doubts me
When I stand for hours
Gazing at you.

THE KISS

Fall not now, petal
Slumber never alone.
Await me to accompany
Till the toxin smothers me
Until then, summon back
The day when existence paused
In an intense moment
- Our first kiss -
In the shades of night.

Remember! Before our kiss
The brook beside dared not gurgle
And warty toad wouldn't croak.
The pansies and the violets woke up
Sensing a scent more exciting than theirs.
The mangoes in the grove dared not swing
And the sparrows in the nest wouldn't shuffle.
The owl and the bat abated their eyes
The clouds in the sky dared not move
And the grazing breeze wouldn't budge.

The moon and the stars peeped about
Sensing a bold move during their reign.
The breath for life laboured heavily,
Heart and soul burned red
Sensing an action nobler than theirs.
Seconds in time wouldn't tick
So as to stall the incident
In a vacuum of time.

Thus in the limelight, our shivering lips
We brought together, to form a pause
In the history of time, so old,
As nature in delight froze.

Remember! After our kiss
The brook which applauded
And the toad who then croaked.
The pansies and the violets whispered
As the doing wafted to them.
The mangoes flushed to ripen
And the sparrows made love.
The owl and the bat gave a secret look
To see if everything was over.

The clouds sulked away
And the breeze blew about.
The moon and the stars stood stoned
That such romance still happened.
The breath continued involuntarily,
Heart and soul calmed themselves
For a moment so prime was over.
Those seconds failed never again

For never alike a moment came
Hitherto in time's eternity.

Now in this candlelight
When my shivering lip
I pout to yours,
So pale and cold,
Lets this nature cease
Forever, for us alone
In the shades of death.

THE PREGNANT GOWN

The gown on the clothesline is pregnant,
That yellow one with flowers embroidered.
Her belly is ballooning, pansies on it are
blooming.

The monsoon gust has come prancing,
Apparently he's now frolicking the frock.
The stalwart gust has forked the fabric.

Appears she is set for eloping,
For their motion are in a rapport now,
And the unclipping is almost done.

Each autumn this guest plays a cameo
And the maverick skims with a pretty apparel.
Last time it was a camisole,
They say he owns a harem.

ENTRUSTING THE SUN TO FIND A BRIDE

Fiery ball of whitened day.
To thee I entrust the duty,
Of finding me a bride of beauty,
To bear me a child so gay.

Sunny as thou should be she
Radiating glory all around.
Tresses of golden hue let surround,
Extruding brightness as of thee.

Let thine journey ever seek,
A lass brown or white,
Black or yellow, of no sect,
But of all, she be meek

Kind sun, brightening ends
Gladden my life too.
Little errand please do
As thou traverse over continents.

HER RIVER BATH

At the brim of the river, she stood
Motionless, to have a dip or not,
While the cold water kissed her feet,
Enticing her to enjoy in him.

Draped in a long plain saree
She stepped into the shallow water
And waded her way as a bride
As his embrace exhilarated her.

Standing alone in depths with awe,
Undid she her silk slowly
And in rushed the frenzy waves
To caress and kiss her breasts.

Inhaling the exotic air of nature
She bowed down into the water.
Coming up, she seemed blessed
As the cold massaged her constitution.

The sun's glare made her blink
In its jealousy against the potamic,
As the swirl ticked her to laughter
While she splashed and spewed on him.

Passing by the river, an urchin
Flipped a pebble at the flirt,
Causing the curves to disappear
Under the protective glittering blanket.

As the interloper walked his way
She hurried up from her pleasure,
But the river echoed her feeling,
We'll unite again in leisure.

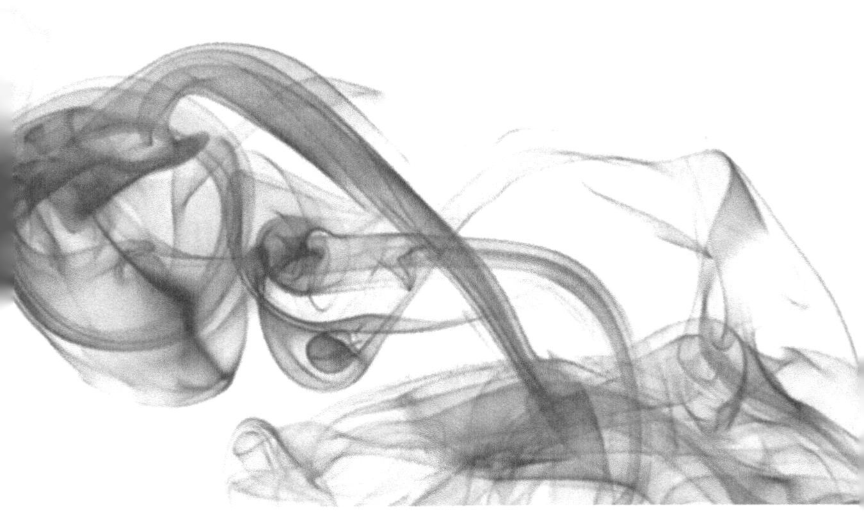

FLYING MACHINE OVER OUR HAMLET

Lately one day, over our hamlet
A machine zoomed with noise so scary.
The laundering crows scurried to their nests
And the frightened cows ran blindly.
The lazy ducks buried their heads in water,
While spotted village dogs chasing anything
Lay huddled in a corner moaning.
The wise old men inhaling the hookah
Under the grand old banyan tree
Trembled. 'It's the end,' they cried.
The village dames, water pots on head,
Spilled the water and drenched
As they stared up quizzically.
A sage in his meditation
Sought with a small eye
'Has God descended so soon?'
A man with a head-spinning cocktail
Got back to the shoppe, to thank

For the excellent audio-visual composition.
Only the children in their crafty games,
Fearlessly with their sticks and books
Chased the intruder to the furthest.

Then when all was at peace,
As if after a swirling wind,
People came out numb or murmuring.
'It's a chopper,' said the village teacher.
As a city returnee whispered, 'It's a plane.'
'It's carrying secrets,' said the law man.
'No,' stamped the ex-fighter, 'it's on to fight.'
Someone said it carried people,
And others grumbled, what else then?
Animals?
Thus the quarrel started
Over a flying machine
That zoomed over our hamlet
And might have reached
Its distant destination
Before the battle here ended.

THE MOON ATOP

A moon is on the tree
Man! The moon's half is atop.
After beer, beside tavern
I saw it sailing high
And on crossing the bridge
I saw it swimming down
Now it's atop
Perching lightly on the tree
Ward her off, shoo her off.
Throw her down, bring her down,
Before she devours our yellow mangoes.
Take this pebble, friend,
Your opportunity let it be
Your miss will be my win
By five mugs of beer,
'Cause, what you don't see
Of that once round egg,
I had brought down yesterday.

HEY MOSQUITO !

It's a pity, it's sad
Tiny little dragons,
To whistle in my ears,
Then stab me innocent,
To drink my gifted blood
And leave a sore behind.

Sleep for which I pray is lost,
Blood for which I labour is stolen,
Skin for which I care is damaged.
Your wish to live, I understand
Or you are extinct,
But then I too have to live
And I have to sleep too.

So then let there be a compromise.
Stealthily steal my blood
After sleep fondles me
So that your stab is not known.
Drink then as much
But don't drain me to death,
For I've got a morrow
But a thing of compulsion is
Don't seek permission before
Nor say thanks after,
Mind you, don't just whistle
In my little sensitive ears
For I am fed up of slapping myself.

OF CUNNING

He was so cunning.
His smile crafted cunningly,
His eyes sporting cunningness,
His ears stretched cunningfully,
His tongue pointed, so cunningfull.

He was so cunning
All knew he lived cunningly,
So cautioned his cunningness.
Thus he who lived cunningfully
Couldn't ever be, so cunningfull.

BHARTI'S PRAYER

A runner did come
From the wiggling ghats' end
To convey me a message, secret.
I pray,
Let the moon wane, wane, wane.
For when the moon gets dissolved
And nobody sees anything,
My immaculate lover in confinement
Will cut those barrier bars
Caging him for years long,
Paining me all the time.

On that blind night
When my lover gathers freedom,
Unknown to those who cursed him in,
I'll pray,
Let the moon wax, wax, wax.
For when the moon matures once more,
Imitating the bright big sun,
Will my lover advent, traversing
Mountains wild and valleys illegible,
To offer me a kiss long sought
Under the Heaven's basking glory.

LIFE AND DEATH

-TWINs

Lay there Mother Earth
In an agony of pleasure
For a child was due
After the longest of penance.
Joy in eyes, pride in heart
She said, Life is his name

And so Life was born
Rosy and beautiful,
Smiling, with eyes sparkling.
(A child of such perfection)
With his first breath
Sprang the nature green.
Flowers bloomed, streams flowed,
Birds chirped, creatures moved.

But smoothness of parturition
Did interrupt much to dismay.
Life's lower limbs stuck,
Seemed the womb was tugging.
Exerted all pressure, mother,
To help her little child out,
And for freedom the child pulled.
A limb got free, then the other
After a battle so weary.

But, but, something more it seemed.
A wrinkled hairy hand grasped
That tender leg so smooth.
A lean warty figure was emerging.
Mother Earth's joy was escalated
For a second child was due.
But worried as happy was she
For an imp was her second child.
His face was wrinkled, nose twisted,
Lips burnt, eyes sunk.
The body's work was such,
An untalented sculptor
In a careless hour would chisel
A figure better than this.
Thus was Death born.

Drowned in sorrow, mother
Named her newer child 'Death'.
As Death blinked his eyes
At the brightened light of day,
Shadows growled, jealousy crept,
Diseases unfolded, disasters leapt.

So Life and Death born together,
Same day, same moment,
Grew under a mother so caring.
But seemed to Death at times
That mother cared for Life more
And to him she hesitated.
Nature hailed and prayed to Life
While on Death they frowned.
Thus jealousy formed a maelstrom
In a soul kept aloof.
Set he pranks against Life
And pelted diseases, tripped to disasters
His brother Life, so pleasant.
Trails of Life, Death followed,
Unknown, silent, at a distance.

Flowers bloomed, young leaves sprouted,
Rivers gurgled, trees waved
As Life walked amidst, whistling.
But his follower's stealthy tread
Made flowers wither, leaves fall,
Rivers parch, trees burn.
Pranks against Life got gruesome
But virtue of patience Life had in him.
This no retaliation angered Death
To reach nadir, to murder.

To murder his brother, so simple,
And it would all be his.
His mother, nature, everything.
All his alone for his happiness.
Thus he laughed till light fainted

And a plot was woven with darkness
Accompanied by shadow for the assault.
They sent the moon on errand
And the stars on a compulsory leave.
Darkness painted the night blacker
To suit the complexion of Death.
No witness to fear, all set,
They set to accomplish the murder,
To demolish Life.

Life in company of blissful nature,
Dancing among swaying flowers,
Singing with chirping birds
Didn't notice the fading light.
Late dark, Life said bye to friends
And nature waved back to the blessed.
He sensed some danger lurking,
Death's another ploy, he knew.
He walked forwards boldly to home
For fear won't help him reach there.

The attitude of game had changed,
Death had unveiled himself, he knew not.
About his mother he thought
And then about the heavenly bodies
Whose absence made world dark
Fumbling, straining along the path,
Suddenly he was pushed towards
A bed of thorns eagerly piercing.
As Life knelt up to walk again,
Death lurking, treading in stealth,
Kissing his dagger 'Fate'

Stabbed Life from behind.
He stabbed Life endlessely,
Making him groan in pain
While he, Death, seizured with joy.

Knowing that Life no more existed,
Rest of the night, in darkness's company
With his servant shadow
He bathed in wine celebrating

Early next day, mother Earth saw
Drooping flowers, withered leaves,
Dried streams, barren mountains,
Dead trees, fallen creatures.
Nature so nursed was dead.

Unwillingly suspecting the worst
Frantic search for Life began.
No answer jaded her
Till she stumbled upon Life's body.
She cried aloud, tore her apparel,
Fell to the ground, beat her head.
Heaping sand on her face,
She muttered a curse on Death
Dipped in agony and pain.
"A good one you killed,
Then let boredom accompany you
To pain you till the end.'

Death for days few roamed
As a king should, till realising,
To admire his ways were none.

He loitered the desert through,
Nothing to do, nothing around,
His mother's curse creeping behind.
He thought of days previous
Troubling Life for entertainment,
Plundering, killing nature for pleasure,
As and when to his will.
He ran away from the curse,
Tried to fight it, then bribe it,
But boredom endured still.
Weary of doing nothing
To defeat boredom, the foe,
He beat out darkness
And little by little
Burnt his servant shadow,
But boredom crept back.

At last, no one to turn to
Nothing else to spend on,
Agonised, angry, cheated,
He took the knife 'Fate'
Which saw the entrails of Life.
And then he stabbed himself
Till blood splattered the land.
As he lay there bleeding
He heard his mother's voice,
'You killed Life, you've learnt,
You, Death, is irrelevant without Life.'
As Death closed his eyes
He heard the echoing laugh,
That of Life's.

NEFFRETTI

Arabia's eastern coast,
Year nineteen seventy three,
Early seventh month,
A mermaid lay still.
A mermaid?

A woman in vessel
Drowns the whole,
For sea loves women,
Else, she be sacrificed
To pacify him, The Poseidon.
Thus believed yester farers
Journeying at nature's mercy.

A woman in vessel
Drowns the whole,
For sea loves women,
Else, she be sacrificed
To pacify him, The Poseidon.
Thus believed yester farers
Journeying at nature's mercy.

Neffretti, pretty sea-side lass,
Clad in happiness
Blessed with laughter
Was fathered by Captain
Of largest vessel - Augustus,
Buoyant in blue Aegean.
Journeying b'ween shores
Of Asia Minor territory
He sought a groom
For his pretty, slender girl.
And when he found
A suitable match,
Asked his daughter
To be ready for journey,
To the Ottoman land
Where life anew awaited.

Thus, on tide high
Proud Augustus sailed
With a beautiful bride,
Guided by constellations,
Breeze and currents.
But men on vessel
Behind hardy hearts

Feared the giant Azure
For amongst was a woman,
Fair and lovely,
Whom Poseidon so craved.
The vessel glided tiptoe,
Captain using skills learnt
Lest he woke the slumbering giant.
Sailors on deck prayed
Even the atheist,
Who cursed the heaven.
But aroma of a woman,
young, lively, beautiful,
Never could be masked
From the women-crazy sea.

Poseidon's awakening
Was heralded by hurrying clouds
Abstaining stars, hiding moon,
And a raging tempest.
Directionless went Augustus,
Helpless stood mariners
Sails tore, masts fell
As sea rose to prey.
Prayers went unheard
Skill proved vain.
'Why me for a woman?'
A question rose by deck
And then another rose,
A mutiny was on.

Captain tried to command
Then gave in to pleadings.

But to no avail amongst sailors
The bride had to be sacrificed
On the altar of lust
Seeing her father confounded
Neffretti came along
Ready to sacrifice herself.
Her father objected
But she persisted.
Sailors stood silent
For they loved her
But not more than their lives.
A sad father, weak captain
Ordered the proceedings
And strode away weeping.

Stripped of her velvet attire
To the bow of Augustus
She was tied firmly.
And the night was chilly.
Sailors withdrew in remorse
Elements slowly calmed,
As Poseidon possessed Neffretti,
An innocent little virgin.
Early morning, amongst
The sea-fowls' cries
A wailing father was heard.
Over a still Neffretti.
He lamented till
The sun reached its zenith,
With vengeance
The captain rose
To order the giant

'If it's women you need
Take this what you spoiled
My very own daughter.
Lo! Her face enchanting
You will not see
But of a fish
As around you.
For the rest of her life
Possess her whensoever
And forever
But never again ever
Should you tear a sail
Or frighten a seaman
For want of a woman.

Sailors then in order
Prayed and paid respects
To a lass named Neffretti
Who saved a vessel
And many more to come.
They shoved her into the blue
And a whirlpool swallowed her,
Pulling her down, to benthos

Ships have sailed safe since
And on every ship's bow
They put a bust of Neffretti
Remembering a sacrifice,
Also reminding Poseidon
Of the order from a captain pained.

Years passed, centuries later,
Arabia's eastern coast,
Year nineteen seventy three,
Early seventh month,
A mermaid lay still.
A mermaid?
Upper body, a fish it was
With fins and scales.
Lower body, a woman it was
For every feature,
Believe, just a woman.

TEMPTATION
FINALE

Lucifer (beguiling)
"Am the omnipotent
Swaying all authority,
Not thy father.
Am the omniscient
Bearing all knowledge,
Not thou.
Am the omnipresent
E'er present everywhere,
Not that spirit.
Am omnificent,
None else.
Am omnifarious,
Me alone.
Worship me now."

"B'come my omen,
Lo! Kingdom below is thine.
B'come my ombudsman,
Aye! Whole world is thine.
B'come my omega,
Nay! Even stars are thine."

Son (potently)
"Away you, ominous.
Away from me omitted,
Always the kingdom was mine
And to kneel before
A father I own."

THE GLADIATOR

In those days, many a beast bled
When his glittering sword pierced
And the crowd had cheered him.
In those days, many a warrior froze
Under his net and three-pronged spear
And the audience had applauded him.
He had his flesh endangered
To delight with his skill
The noblest of all, the Romans.

But now a foe named age
Has lessened his lightning spirit
And made him fumble in tactics,
Enough for his young opponent
To find the Gladiator's entrails.

Fallen now he has in arena,
That same Rome for whom
He had devoted his life
Cried and fancied for his blood,
For it mattered never to Romans
Whose blood that gave them mirth
As long as its colour was red.

Around the Gladiator rose heinous cries,
Petals and ribbons brimmed the theatre.
The eternal Caesar wriggled impatiently
For the delay in fulfilling a task.
Someone of his train spoke
For the inevitable to be quicker.

As the hero brought up his sword
The gathering gave a joyful shriek
And the lost warrior a whimper.
When the sharpened point landed again
The nobles were pleased for the day.

As he lay there bleeding, the Gladiator,
Devoted blood drenching the Roman Soil,
His lips must have muttered a curse
For the betrayal done to him.

THE TRIMITRI COAST

Lay the Trimitri coast calm
A lighthouse towering to boast,
Shedding streaks of hope at dark
Saying, 'A land to weary is here.'

Galleys on trade at sun's demise
Prayed for Trimitri's guidance.
Thanked they in mind the old watch
For his unfailing call to duty.

A thundery day, the grey beard watched
Gulls flee, clouds scurry,
Sea slashing, wind hammering.
'Heaven has helled,' yelled the watch.

Raging tempest, hurling rain,
Raging thunder, spearing lightning,
Quivering earth, gashing coast.
Crumbled lay pride, light of Trimitri.

Horrified old, sheltered by a cave
Aside the looming cliff spying coast,
Saw in a flash a mastless ship tossing,
Graspless how or where to head.

'Let death not intrude, sailors be saved,'
Prayed in earnest the old beard.
Shouted he though feeble, waved though frail
To no avail, in peril was the vessel.

Deep in cave a flicker he saw
Although his eyes swelled in tears.
Then a shimmer in his cerebrum,
For that was the lone way.

Not a hundred, a thou crisscrossed,
Yes! Those little warm glow worms.
Collected he many into his blown out lantern
And sped to the top of the cliff.

And there emitted a green radiance,
A path of hope to those in peril.
Brighter it was than once lighted tower
And saved many at the Trimitri's coast.

Sailors in havoc, still today,
Call upon the old watch's spirit,
As should be believed, up on the cliff it
Appears with that green radiance of hope.

YUDDAN

"The most beautiful for me,
Only the fairest of them."
Kneeling on the bank
Staring into the river
Which he had harnessed
He whispered impatiently.

He knelt there till his
Virtual image was etched
On the stagnant speculum river
By the above glaring sun.
"Take my picture along lands
Till you see a face glowing.
Show her then my inspiring face,
For sure will she love it.

Imprint her face as she'd gaze
And carry it back to me, fast.
Then will I go aplomb for her."
"Go, go, little river
Do this bit for me,"
Saying so he unbridled the river
Which surged forward gay.
It went yonder mountains,
Thro' valleys, across woods,
Along towns, 'neath bridges

Besides groves, 'gainst hurdles.
It ran with a face,
One so charming.
Then it crossed a village
Where a belle bearing vessel
Collected her evening pail.
Enchanted the river was
And in love the lass was
With the catoptric face,
Bewitching, charismatic.
Not of the potamic
The lass never knew,
As she ogled in abstractedness.
Its errand, the river forgot
On seeing such a sanguine face,
Insipid were others to this countenance.
Glittering back the rays of sun
Into her long little eyes
The river did hypnotise her.
In a trance she walked deep
And the river with her, galloped off.

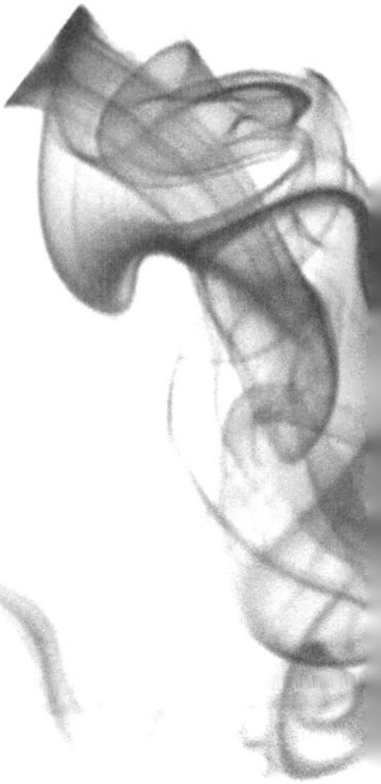

As for Yuddan, he awaited days
On a riparian black rock
-Fervent, fervid, fervour -
Till someone passing said,
'River flows only forward.'

THE CROSSING OVER OF MOTHER TERESA

I heard the bugles trill
Of those men in drill
For a woman having nil
Because she did toil and till
Finishing her job as His will.

(The crossing over)

I hear the bugles thrill,
Seem from a distant hill
Beside some exquisite rill,
By angels in cloaks with frill
As her name is entered with a quill.